THE ART OF INSPIRING LEADERSHIP

LEADERSHIP

A Guide to Developing a Vision
and Mission for Success

Attila Rinderman

CONTENTS

INTRODUCTION

Leadership is a crucial component of success in any organization, and being a great leader is a skill that can be developed through practice and dedication. However, leadership is not just about managing tasks, but about inspiring and guiding your team towards success. As a leader, you have the opportunity to make a positive impact on the lives of those around you and the organizations you work with.

In this book, we will explore the key principles and strategies for becoming a great leader. We will cover a wide range of topics, from developing a strong vision and mission, to building trust and creating a positive culture, to managing time and priorities, to leading in times of crisis. We will also delve into the importance of emotional intelligence, effective communication, and continuous learning and development.

Whether you are a new leader or an experienced one, there is always room for improvement. By incorporating the strategies outlined in this book into your leadership approach, you can become a more effective and successful leader. You will learn how to build strong relationships with your team, create a culture of accountability, celebrate success, and foster diversity and inclusion.

Throughout this book, we will provide practical tips and real-world examples of how to apply these principles in your daily life as a leader. We will also discuss the challenges that come with leadership and how to overcome them.

Ultimately, our goal is to help you become a leader who inspires and motivates your team to achieve their full potential. With the right mindset and approach, you can become a great leader who makes a positive impact on those around you and drives success for your organization.

CHAPTER 1: DEVELOPING
A STRONG VISION AND MISSION

Developing a strong vision and mission is the foundation of effective leadership. A clear and inspiring vision and mission can guide your team towards a shared goal and provide a sense of purpose and direction. In this chapter, we'll explore the key components of a strong vision and mission and how to develop them for your organization.

What is a Vision Statement?

A vision statement is a statement that outlines the future state or long-term goal of an organization. It is a vivid and inspiring description of where the organization is heading and what it hopes to achieve. A vision statement should be concise, memorable, and communicate the values and aspirations of the organization.

Why is a Vision Statement Important?

A strong vision statement can motivate and inspire your team towards a shared goal. It can also help you make decisions that align with the long-term direction of the organization. A clear and compelling vision statement can also attract and retain talented employees who share your values and aspirations.

How to Develop a Vision Statement?

Developing a vision statement requires thoughtful reflection and discussion. Here are some steps to follow:

1   Gather input from stakeholders: Start by gathering input from your team, customers, and other stakeholders. Ask them what they see as the long-term goals and aspirations of the organization. This feedback can help you identify common themes and values that can inform your vision statement.

2   Identify your core values: Your vision statement should be rooted in your organization's core values. Identify the values that are most important to your organization and that you want to guide your decision-making and behavior.

3   Envision the future: Once you have identified your core values, envision the future state of your organization. What does success look like? What are the long-term goals and aspirations that will guide your organization towards this future state?

4   Write a draft: Use the insights and feedback gathered from stakeholders to draft a clear and inspiring vision statement. Keep it concise and memorable, and make sure it communicates the values and aspirations of your organization.

5   Refine and communicate: Share your vision statement with your team and stakeholders and gather feedback. Refine it as needed, and communicate it regularly to ensure everyone is aligned and working towards the same goal.

What is a Mission Statement?

A mission statement is a statement that outlines the purpose and objectives of an organization. It describes the products or services the organization provides, its target customers or stakeholders, and the values and principles that guide its operations. A mission statement should be clear, concise, and inspiring.

Why is a Mission Statement Important?

A strong mission statement can provide a sense of purpose and direction for your team. It can also help you make decisions that align with the values and objectives of the organization. A clear and compelling mission statement can also attract and retain customers and stakeholders who share your values and principles.

How to Develop a Mission Statement?

Developing a mission statement requires a similar approach to developing a vision statement. Here are some steps to follow:

1   Define your products or services: Start by defining the products or services your organization provides. What are the unique features and benefits that set your organization apart from others?

2   Identify your target customers or stakeholders: Who are the customers or stakeholders that your organization serves? What are their needs and aspirations?

3   Define your values and principles: Identify the values and principles that guide your organization's operations. What are the ethical and moral standards that you uphold in your work?

4   Write a draft: Use the insights and feedback gathered from stakeholders to draft a clear and inspiring mission statement. Keep it concise and memorable, and make sure it communicates the purpose and objectives of your organization.

5   Refine and communicate: Share your mission statement with your team and stakeholders and gather feedback. Refine it as needed, and communicate it regularly to ensure everyone is aligned and working towards the same purpose.

The Importance of Aligning Vision and Mission

Your organization's vision and mission should be aligned to ensure that they work together to guide your team towards a shared goal. Your vision statement should provide the big picture of where you want to go, while your mission statement should provide the specific actions you will take to achieve that vision. When these two statements are aligned, they can inspire and guide your team towards a shared goal.

In addition to aligning your vision and mission statements, it's important to ensure that they are also aligned with your organization's values and culture. When these elements are aligned, they can create a sense of purpose and direction that can motivate and inspire your team.

Conclusion

Developing a strong vision and mission is an essential component of effective leadership. A clear and inspiring vision and mission can guide your team towards a shared goal and provide a sense of purpose and direction. By following the steps outlined in this chapter, you can develop a vision and mission statement that aligns with your organization's values and aspirations, and inspires and guides your team towards success. Remember to regularly communicate your vision and mission to ensure everyone is aligned and working towards the same purpose.

CHAPTER 2: SETTING
GOALS AND OBJECTIVES

Once you have developed a strong vision and mission for your organization, the next step is to set clear and measurable goals and objectives that can help you achieve that vision. Goals and objectives provide the roadmap for your team, helping them focus their efforts and resources towards the most important outcomes. In this chapter, we'll explore the key components of effective goal setting and how to develop goals and objectives that can motivate and guide your team towards success.

What are Goals and Objectives?

Goals are broad statements of what you want to achieve, while objectives are specific and measurable targets that support those goals. Goals are the "what" of your vision and mission, while objectives are the "how" that can help you achieve those goals. Both goals and objectives should be specific, measurable, attainable, relevant, and time-bound (SMART).

Why are Goals and Objectives Important?

Goals and objectives provide the framework for achieving your vision and mission. They help you focus your team's efforts and resources on the most important outcomes, and provide a clear and measurable way to track progress and success. By setting goals and objectives, you can ensure that your team is aligned and working towards a common goal.

How to Set Effective Goals and Objectives?

Effective goal setting requires a thoughtful and deliberate approach. Here are some steps to follow:

1   Review your vision and mission: Start by reviewing your vision and mission statements. What are the long-term goals and aspirations that you want to achieve? What are the specific outcomes that will help you achieve those goals?

2   Identify key performance indicators: Identify the key performance indicators (KPIs) that will help you measure progress towards your goals. These should be specific and measurable metrics that will tell you whether you're on track to achieve your objectives.

3   Set specific and measurable objectives: Based on your KPIs, set specific and measurable objectives that will support your goals. Make sure they are relevant to your vision and mission, and attainable within the timeframe you have set.

4   Break down objectives into tasks: Break down each objective into specific tasks that need to be completed to achieve them. These tasks should be assigned to specific team members, and have clear deadlines and deliverables.

5   Assign responsibility and accountability: Assign responsibility and accountability for each objective and task to specific team members. Make sure they understand their roles and responsibilities, and have the necessary resources and support to achieve their objectives.

6   Monitor progress and adjust as needed: Monitor progress towards your objectives and adjust your plans as needed. Regularly review your KPIs and adjust your objectives and tasks to ensure you're on track to achieve your goals.

Examples of Goals and Objectives

Here are some examples of goals and objectives that can help you achieve your vision and mission:

Goal: Increase customer satisfaction

Objective 1: Improve response time to customer inquiries by 50% within 3 months

Objective 2: Increase the number of positive customer reviews by 20% within 6 months

Objective 3: Implement a customer loyalty program that increases repeat business by 30% within 1 year

Goal: Increase revenue

Objective 1: Launch a new product line that generates $100,000 in revenue within 6 months

Objective 2: Increase sales of existing products by 15% within 9 months

Objective 3: Expand into a new market that generates $50,000 in revenue within 1 year

Goal: Improve employee engagement

Objective 1: Conduct a company-wide employee survey and implement feedback within 3 months

Objective 2: Increase the number of employee-led initiatives by 50% within 6 months

Objective 3: Implement a professional development program that improves employee retention by 20% within 1 year

Conclusion

Setting effective goals and objectives is a critical component of achieving your vision and mission. By following the steps outlined in this chapter, you can develop specific, measurable, attainable, relevant, and time-bound (SMART) goals and objectives that will guide your team towards success. Remember to regularly monitor progress towards your objectives and adjust your plans as needed to ensure you're on track to achieve your goals. With the right approach and a clear roadmap, you can achieve your organization's vision and mission, and make a positive impact on the world.

CHAPTER 3: BUILDING
TRUST AND CREDIBILITY

Building trust and credibility is a critical component of effective leadership. Trust is the foundation of strong relationships, and credibility is essential for building confidence and inspiring others. In this chapter, we'll explore the key principles of building trust and credibility, and how to develop strong relationships with your team and stakeholders.

What is Trust?

Trust is the belief or confidence that one person has in another person or group. It is the foundation of strong relationships and is essential for effective leadership. When trust is present, people are more willing to take risks, share ideas, and work together towards a common goal.

Why is Trust Important?

Trust is important in leadership for several reasons. First, it provides the foundation for strong relationships with your team and stakeholders. When people trust you, they are more likely to follow your lead and support your decisions. Second, trust is essential for effective communication. When people trust you, they are more likely to listen to what you have to say and take your feedback seriously. Finally, trust is critical for innovation and risk-taking. When people trust you, they are more likely to take risks and try new things, which can lead to new and innovative solutions.

How to Build Trust?

Building trust requires a deliberate and intentional approach. Here are some steps to follow:

1   Be honest and transparent: Honesty and transparency are essential for building trust. Be honest about your intentions and motivations, and communicate openly and transparently with your team and stakeholders.
2   Follow through on commitments: When you make a commitment, follow through on it. This demonstrates your reliability and builds trust with your team and stakeholders.
3   Listen actively: Actively listening to your team and stakeholders demonstrates that you value their opinions and perspectives. This can help build trust and foster strong relationships.
4   Admit mistakes and take responsibility: Admitting mistakes and taking responsibility demonstrates that you are accountable for your actions. This can build trust and credibility with your team and stakeholders.
5   Keep confidences: Keeping confidences demonstrates that you are trustworthy and can be relied upon to protect sensitive information.
6   Show respect and empathy: Showing respect and empathy towards your team and stakeholders can help build trust and foster strong relationships. When people feel respected and understood, they are more likely to trust you and work together towards a common goal.

What is Credibility?

Credibility is the quality of being believable or trustworthy. It is essential for effective leadership, as it can inspire confidence and inspire others to follow your lead. Credibility is based on a combination of your actions, words, and reputation.

Why is Credibility Important?

Credibility is important in leadership for several reasons. First, it can inspire confidence in your team and stakeholders. When people believe in you, they are more likely to follow your lead and support your decisions. Second, credibility is essential for effective communication. When people believe that you are knowledgeable and trustworthy, they are more likely to listen to what you have to say and take your feedback seriously. Finally, credibility can help build your reputation as a leader. When people see you as credible and trustworthy, they are more likely to recommend you to others and help you build your network and influence.

How to Build Credibility?

Building credibility requires a deliberate and intentional approach. Here are some steps to follow:

1. Demonstrate expertise: Demonstrating expertise in your field can help build credibility with your team and stakeholders. This can include pursuing professional development, staying up-to-date with industry trends, and sharing your knowledge and insights with others.
2. Communicate clearly and effectively: Clear and effective communication can help build credibility with your team and stakeholders. Make sure you are communicating in a way that is easy to understand and relevant to your audience.
3. Build a strong track record: Building a strong track record of success can help build credibility. This can include achieving results, meeting targets and deadlines, and delivering on commitments.
4. Develop a strong network: Developing a strong network of contacts can help build credibility by demonstrating that you have support and connections within your industry.
5. Embrace feedback: Embracing feedback and using it to

improve can demonstrate your openness to growth and development, which can help build credibility with your team and stakeholders.

6   Be consistent: Consistency in your actions, words, and behavior can help build credibility by demonstrating that you are reliable and can be counted on to deliver.

Conclusion

Building trust and credibility is an essential component of effective leadership. By following the steps outlined in this chapter, you can develop strong relationships with your team and stakeholders, and inspire confidence and trust. Remember to be honest and transparent, follow through on commitments, listen actively, admit mistakes and take responsibility, keep confidences, show respect and empathy, demonstrate expertise, communicate clearly and effectively, build a strong track record, develop a strong network, embrace feedback, and be consistent. With these principles in mind, you can build trust and credibility, and lead your team to success.

CHAPTER 4: EFFECTIVE
COMMUNICATION IN LEADERSHIP

Effective communication is essential for effective leadership. It's the cornerstone of building trust, fostering strong relationships, and achieving your vision and mission. In this chapter, we'll explore the key principles of effective communication, and how to communicate in a way that inspires, motivates, and guides your team towards success.

What is Effective Communication?

Effective communication is the process of exchanging information and ideas in a way that is easy to understand, relevant to the audience, and achieves the desired outcome. It involves the use of verbal and nonverbal communication, as well as active listening and feedback.

Why is Effective Communication Important?

Effective communication is important in leadership for several reasons. First, it provides the foundation for building strong relationships with your team and stakeholders. When you communicate effectively, you can build trust, demonstrate credibility, and inspire confidence in your leadership. Second, effective communication is essential for achieving your vision and mission. When you communicate clearly and consistently, you can ensure that your team is aligned and working towards a common goal. Finally, effective communication is critical for problem-solving and conflict resolution. When you communicate openly and honestly, you can resolve conflicts and find solutions to complex problems.

How to Communicate Effectively?

Communicating effectively requires a thoughtful and intentional approach. Here are some steps to follow:

1   Understand your audience: To communicate effectively, you need to understand your audience. This includes their needs, preferences, and communication styles. Take the time to listen to your team and stakeholders, and tailor your communication to their needs.

2   Be clear and concise: Clarity and conciseness are essential for effective communication. Make sure your message is easy to understand, and avoid using jargon or technical language that may confuse your audience.

3   Use active listening: Active listening involves paying attention to your audience, asking questions, and seeking clarification. This can help you understand their needs and concerns, and tailor your communication to their needs.

4   Provide feedback: Providing feedback is essential for effective communication. This can include both positive feedback to reinforce good behavior and negative feedback to correct behavior that needs improvement. Make sure your feedback is specific, actionable, and delivered in a way that is respectful and constructive.

5   Use nonverbal communication: Nonverbal communication, such as body language and tone of voice, can convey a lot of information. Make sure your nonverbal communication is consistent with your verbal communication, and conveys the intended message.

6   Be consistent: Consistency in your communication is essential for building trust and credibility. Make sure your message is consistent over time, and avoid sending mixed messages that may confuse or frustrate your audience.

Examples of Effective Communication

Here are some examples of effective communication that can help you achieve your vision and mission:

1   Town hall meetings: Town hall meetings can be an effective way to communicate with your team and stakeholders. These meetings provide a forum for open and transparent communication, and allow you to address concerns and answer questions in real-time.

2   One-on-one meetings: One-on-one meetings with team members can be an effective way to provide feedback and build strong relationships. These meetings can provide a forum for active listening, feedback, and problem-solving.

3   Performance reviews: Performance reviews can be an effective way to provide feedback, set goals and objectives, and recognize achievements. These reviews can help you communicate your expectations and provide guidance for improvement.

4   Newsletters: Newsletters can be an effective way to communicate with your team and stakeholders on a regular basis. These newsletters can provide updates on progress towards your goals and objectives, recognize achievements, and communicate important information.

Conclusion

Effective communication is essential for effective leadership. By following the steps outlined in this chapter, you can communicate in a way that inspires, motivates, and guides your team towards success. Remember to understand your audience, be clear and concise, use active listening, provide feedback, use nonverbal communication, and be consistent. With these principles in mind, you can build strong relationships with your team and stakeholders, achieve your vision and mission, and make a positive impact on the world. Effective communication is not only important for achieving success in the short term, but it is also a critical skill for personal and professional growth in the long term.

CHAPTER 5:
DEVELOPING A POSITIVE ORGANIZATIONAL CULTURE

Organizational culture refers to the shared values, beliefs, and practices that shape the behavior and attitudes of an organization's members. A positive organizational culture can inspire and motivate employees, foster innovation and creativity, and contribute to the achievement of the organization's goals. In this chapter, we'll explore the key principles of a positive organizational culture, and how to develop and maintain a culture that can lead to success.

What is Organizational Culture?

Organizational culture is the shared values, beliefs, and practices that shape the behavior and attitudes of an organization's members. It includes the organization's mission and vision, as well as its policies, procedures, and practices. Organizational culture can have a significant impact on the behavior and performance of employees, as well as the organization's overall success.

Why is Organizational Culture Important?

Organizational culture is important for several reasons. First, a positive organizational culture can inspire and motivate employees, and foster a sense of belonging and community. This can lead to increased job satisfaction, engagement, and productivity. Second, a positive organizational culture can promote innovation and creativity by encouraging employees to share ideas and take risks. Finally, a positive organizational culture can contribute to the achievement of the organization's goals by aligning employees' behaviors and attitudes with the organization's mission and vision.

How to Develop a Positive Organizational Culture?

Developing a positive organizational culture requires a deliberate and intentional approach. Here are some steps to follow:

1   Define your organization's values: Start by defining your organization's values. What are the core beliefs and principles that guide your organization's behavior and decision-making? Make sure these values are aligned with your mission and vision, and communicate them clearly to your team.

2   Hire for culture fit: When hiring new employees, make sure they are a good fit for your organization's culture. This can include looking for candidates who share your organization's values and have a positive attitude.

3   Encourage open communication: Encourage open communication and feedback within your organization. This can help build trust and foster a sense of community, and can also lead to innovation and creativity.

4   Recognize and reward good behavior: Recognize and reward employees who exhibit behaviors that align with your organization's values. This can include recognizing employees who go above and beyond their job duties, or who exhibit behaviors that contribute to a positive organizational culture.

5   Provide opportunities for growth and development: Provide opportunities for growth and development, such as training and development programs, mentoring, and coaching. This can help employees develop new skills and improve their performance, which can contribute to a

positive organizational culture.

6   Lead by example: Finally, lead by example. Model the behaviors and attitudes you want to see in your organization, and hold yourself and others accountable for upholding your organization's values.

Examples of a Positive Organizational Culture

Here are some examples of a positive organizational culture that can lead to success:

1   Google: Google is known for its innovative and collaborative culture. The company encourages employees to share ideas and take risks, and provides opportunities for growth and development.
2   Zappos: Zappos is known for its customer-centric culture, which emphasizes the importance of customer satisfaction. The company encourages employees to go above and beyond to meet customer needs, and provides a fun and engaging work environment.
3   Southwest Airlines: Southwest Airlines is known for its positive and fun culture, which emphasizes the importance of employee engagement and satisfaction. The company provides opportunities for growth and development, and emphasizes the importance of teamwork and collaboration.

Conclusion

Developing a positive organizational culture is an essential component of achieving success. By following the steps outlined in this chapter, you can develop a culture that inspires and motivates employees, fosters innovation and creativity, and contributes to the achievement of your organization's goals. Remember to define your organization's values, hire for culture fit, encourage open communication, recognize and reward good behavior, provide opportunities for growth and development, and lead by example. With these principles in mind, you can develop and maintain a positive organizational culture that can lead to success in the short and long term.

CHAPTER 6: LEADING
TEAMS EFFECTIVELY

Leading teams effectively is an essential component of effective leadership. Whether you're leading a small team or a large organization, the ability to inspire and motivate your team can make a significant difference in achieving your vision and mission. In this chapter, we'll explore the key principles of leading teams effectively, and how to develop a high-performing team that can achieve success.

What is Team Leadership?

Team leadership is the ability to inspire and motivate a group of individuals towards a common goal. It involves the ability to communicate effectively, provide guidance and support, and create a positive and engaging work environment. Team leadership can have a significant impact on the performance and success of an organization.

Why is Team Leadership Important?

Team leadership is important for several reasons. First, it provides the foundation for building a high-performing team. When employees are motivated and engaged, they are more likely to work together towards a common goal and achieve success. Second, team leadership can promote innovation and creativity by encouraging employees to share ideas and take risks. Finally, team leadership can help create a positive work environment that promotes job satisfaction, retention, and productivity.

How to Lead Teams Effectively?

Leading teams effectively requires a thoughtful and intentional approach. Here are some steps to follow:

1.   Establish clear goals and expectations: Establish clear goals and expectations for your team, and communicate them clearly. Make sure your team understands what they are working towards, and how their work contributes to the organization's vision and mission.

2.   Communicate effectively: Communicate effectively with your team, and provide feedback and guidance as needed. Make sure your communication is clear and relevant, and that your team understands what is expected of them.

3.   Develop a positive work environment: Develop a positive work environment that promotes engagement, motivation, and productivity. This can include providing opportunities for growth and development, recognizing and rewarding good behavior, and creating a culture of open communication.

4.   Empower your team: Empower your team to take ownership of their work and make decisions. This can help build trust and foster a sense of ownership, which can lead to increased engagement and motivation.

5.   Lead by example: Lead by example, and model the behaviors and attitudes you want to see in your team. This can include demonstrating a positive attitude, working collaboratively, and taking ownership of your work.

6.   Encourage teamwork and collaboration: Encourage teamwork and collaboration within your team, and provide opportunities for team building and collaboration. This can help build trust and foster a sense of community, which can lead to increased engagement and motivation.

Examples of Effective Team Leadership

Here are some examples of effective team leadership that can lead to success:

1   Steve Jobs: Steve Jobs was known for his ability to inspire and motivate his team towards a common goal. He was a visionary leader who communicated his vision effectively and provided guidance and support to his team.

2   Oprah Winfrey: Oprah Winfrey is known for her ability to create a positive work environment that promotes engagement and motivation. She empowers her team to take ownership of their work and provides opportunities for growth and development.

3   Pat Summitt: Pat Summitt was a legendary basketball coach who led her team to eight national championships. She was known for her ability to motivate and inspire her team, and for her commitment to teamwork and collaboration.

Conclusion

Leading teams effectively is an essential component of effective leadership. By following the steps outlined in this chapter, you can develop a high-performing team that can achieve success. Remember to establish clear goals and expectations, communicate effectively, develop a positive work environment, empower your team, lead by example, and encourage teamwork and collaboration. With these principles in mind, you can lead your team towards success and achieve your organization's vision and mission.

CHAPTER 7: EMOTIONAL INTELLIGENCE IN LEADERSHIP

Emotional intelligence is a critical component of effective leadership. It involves the ability to understand and manage your own emotions, as well as the emotions of others. In this chapter, we'll explore the key principles of emotional intelligence, and how to develop this essential skill for effective leadership.

What is Emotional Intelligence?

Emotional intelligence is the ability to understand and manage your own emotions, as well as the emotions of others. It involves the ability to recognize and manage your own emotions, as well as the emotions of others, and to use this understanding to guide your behavior and decision-making.

Why is Emotional Intelligence Important?

Emotional intelligence is important for several reasons. First, it helps build strong relationships with your team and stakeholders. When you understand and manage your own emotions, you can communicate more effectively, build trust, and inspire confidence in your leadership. Second, emotional intelligence can help you manage stress and conflict more effectively. When you are aware of your own emotions and how they impact your behavior, you can respond to challenging situations in a more constructive way. Finally, emotional intelligence can promote empathy and understanding, which can help you build a more positive and engaged work environment.

How to Develop Emotional Intelligence?

Developing emotional intelligence requires a thoughtful and intentional approach. Here are some steps to follow:

1   Develop self-awareness: Developing self-awareness involves understanding your own emotions, strengths, and weaknesses. Take the time to reflect on your own emotions and how they impact your behavior, and seek feedback from others to gain a better understanding of how you are perceived.

2   Manage your emotions: Managing your emotions involves controlling your emotions and using them to guide your behavior and decision-making. This can include techniques such as mindfulness, meditation, and deep breathing, as well as seeking support from others when needed.

3   Develop empathy: Developing empathy involves understanding and relating to the emotions of others. This can involve active listening, seeking to understand others' perspectives, and responding to their emotions in a way that is supportive and constructive.

4   Practice effective communication: Effective communication involves the ability to express yourself in a way that is clear, concise, and empathetic. This can involve active listening, asking questions, and seeking feedback to ensure that your message is being understood.

5   Build positive relationships: Building positive relationships involves developing strong connections with your team and stakeholders. This can involve showing empathy, being supportive and respectful, and building trust through consistent and open communication.

Examples of Emotional Intelligence in Leadership

Here are some examples of emotional intelligence in leadership:

1   Bill Gates: Bill Gates is known for his ability to manage his emotions and make effective decisions under pressure. He is

also known for his empathy and ability to connect with his team.

2   Michelle Obama: Michelle Obama is known for her ability to inspire and connect with people from diverse backgrounds. She is also known for her ability to manage stress and adversity with grace and resilience.

3   Richard Branson: Richard Branson is known for his ability to connect with people and build positive relationships. He is also known for his ability to manage his emotions and make bold decisions with confidence.

Conclusion

Developing emotional intelligence is an essential component of effective leadership. By following the steps outlined in this chapter, you can develop this critical skill and become a more effective leader. Remember to develop self-awareness, manage your emotions, develop empathy, practice effective communication, and build positive relationships. With these principles in mind, you can become a more empathetic, understanding, and effective leader, and inspire your team to achieve success.

CHAPTER 8: BUILDING AND
LEADING HIGH-PERFORMING TEAMS

Building and leading high-performing teams is an essential component of effective leadership. A high-performing team can achieve more, innovate more, and have a greater impact than a team that is not performing at its best. In this chapter, we'll explore the key principles of building and leading high-performing teams, and how to develop a team that can achieve success.

What is a High-Performing Team?

A high-performing team is a group of individuals who work together towards a common goal, and consistently achieve high levels of performance. High-performing teams are characterized by high levels of engagement, collaboration, innovation, and productivity.

Why is a High-Performing Team Important?

A high-performing team is important for several reasons. First, it can achieve more than a team that is not performing at its best. When a team is highly engaged and motivated, it is more likely to achieve its goals and have a greater impact. Second, a high-performing team can promote innovation and creativity by encouraging team members to share ideas and take risks. Finally, a high-performing team can contribute to a positive work environment that promotes job satisfaction, retention, and productivity.

How to Build a High-Performing Team?

Building a high-performing team requires a thoughtful and intentional approach. Here are some steps to follow:

1   Define clear goals and expectations: Start by defining clear goals and expectations for your team. Make sure everyone understands what they are working towards, and how their work contributes to the organization's vision and mission.
2   Hire for cultural fit: When hiring new team members, make sure they are a good cultural fit for your team. Look for candidates who share your team's values and have the skills and experience to contribute to your team's success.
3   Foster open communication: Foster open communication within your team by providing opportunities for team members to share ideas, provide feedback, and collaborate. Make sure everyone feels comfortable expressing their opinions and ideas.
4   Build trust: Build trust within your team by demonstrating integrity, consistency, and fairness. Be transparent about your decisions and actions, and hold yourself and your team accountable for achieving your goals.
5   Provide opportunities for growth and development: Provide opportunities for growth and development by investing in training and development programs, mentoring, coaching, and other forms of professional development. This can help team members improve their skills and knowledge, and contribute to the success of your team.
6   Encourage collaboration: Encourage collaboration within your team by providing opportunities for team members to work together on projects, and by recognizing and rewarding teamwork.

Examples of High-Performing Teams

Here are some examples of high-performing teams:

1   Pixar Animation Studios: Pixar Animation Studios is known for its high-performing teams, which produce some of the most successful animated movies in the world. The company fosters a culture of collaboration, creativity, and innovation, and provides opportunities for team members to develop their skills and knowledge.

2   Apple Inc.: Apple Inc. is known for its high-performing teams, which design and develop some of the most innovative products in the world. The company fosters a culture of collaboration and creativity, and provides opportunities for team members to take ownership of their work and contribute to the success of the organization.

3   Google: Google is known for its high-performing teams, which develop some of the most innovative and successful products and services in the world. The company fosters a culture of collaboration, creativity, and innovation, and provides opportunities for team members to develop their skills and knowledge.

Conclusion

Building and leading high-performing teams is an essential component of effective leadership. By following the steps outlined in this chapter, you can develop a team that is engaged, motivated, and productive. Remember to define clear goals and expectations, hire for cultural fit, foster open communication, build trust, provide opportunities for growth and development, and encourage collaboration. With these principles in mind, you can lead your team towards success and achieve your organization's vision and mission. Building and leading a high-performing team takes time, effort, and patience, but the payoff in terms of team performance and overall success is well worth it.

CHAPTER 9:
LEADING CHANGE

Leading change is an essential component of effective leadership. As an organization or team evolves, change is inevitable, and the ability to manage change effectively can have a significant impact on the success of the organization. In this chapter, we'll explore the key principles of leading change, and how to manage change effectively.

What is Change Management?

Change management is the process of preparing and supporting individuals, teams, and organizations in making a change. It involves a structured approach to transitioning individuals and organizations from their current state to a desired future state.

Why is Change Management Important?

Change management is important for several reasons. First, it helps reduce the negative impact of change on individuals and teams. Change can be disruptive and can cause anxiety and stress, and effective change management can help minimize the negative impact on employees. Second, change management can promote innovation and creativity by encouraging individuals and teams to embrace new ways of thinking and working. Finally, change management can help organizations achieve their goals by enabling them to adapt and evolve in response to changing market conditions and customer needs.

How to Lead Change?

Leading change requires a thoughtful and intentional approach. Here are some steps to follow:

1   Define the need for change: Define the need for change by identifying the problem or opportunity that requires change. Make sure everyone understands the need for change and why it is important.
2   Develop a vision for change: Develop a vision for change by defining what the future state will look like. Make sure the vision is clear and compelling, and that everyone understands what they are working towards.
3   Communicate effectively: Communicate the need for change and the vision for change effectively to all stakeholders. Make sure everyone understands why the change is necessary, what the vision is, and what their role is in making the change happen.
4   Develop a plan for change: Develop a plan for change that includes specific steps, timelines, and responsibilities. Make sure the plan is detailed and comprehensive, and that everyone knows what is expected of them.
5   Implement the plan: Implement the plan for change, and monitor progress closely. Make sure everyone is following the plan and that any issues are addressed promptly.
6   Provide support: Provide support to individuals and teams as they go through the change process. This can include providing training, coaching, and other forms of support to help them adapt to the changes.

Examples of Leading Change

Here are some examples of leading change:

1   Steve Jobs: Steve Jobs was known for his ability to lead change at Apple Inc. He was responsible for introducing new products, such as the iPhone and iPad, that transformed the technology industry.

2   Nelson Mandela: Nelson Mandela was known for his ability to lead change in South Africa. He was instrumental in ending apartheid and promoting reconciliation and unity among different groups.

3   Satya Nadella: Satya Nadella, the CEO of Microsoft, has led the company through significant change, including a shift to cloud computing and a focus on innovation and creativity.

Conclusion

Leading change is an essential component of effective leadership. By following the steps outlined in this chapter, you can lead change effectively and achieve your organization's goals. Remember to define the need for change, develop a vision for change, communicate effectively, develop a plan for change, implement the plan, and provide support. With these principles in mind, you can lead your organization towards success and achieve your vision and mission. Leading change takes time, effort, and patience, but the payoff in terms of organizational success is well worth it. Remember that leading change is a process, and it requires ongoing effort and patience. By implementing the principles discussed in this chapter, you can develop and refine your change management skills, and become a more effective leader. With a greater understanding of how to manage change effectively, you can lead your organization towards success and achieve your vision and mission.

CHAPTER 10: LEADING
WITH INTEGRITY

Integrity is a critical component of effective leadership. It involves adhering to a set of values and principles that guide your behavior and decision-making. In this chapter, we'll explore the key principles of leading with integrity, and how to develop and maintain a culture of integrity within your organization.

What is Integrity?

Integrity is the quality of being honest and having strong moral principles. It involves doing the right thing, even when it's difficult, and adhering to a set of values and principles that guide your behavior and decision-making.

Why is Integrity Important?

Integrity is important for several reasons. First, it helps build trust and credibility with your team and stakeholders. When you demonstrate integrity, you inspire confidence in your leadership and create a positive and productive work environment. Second, integrity can promote a culture of accountability and responsibility, where everyone takes ownership of their actions and decisions. Finally, integrity can promote ethical behavior, which can lead to better decision-making and overall organizational success.

How to Lead with Integrity?

Leading with integrity requires a thoughtful and intentional approach. Here are some steps to follow:

1   Define your values and principles: Define your values and principles by identifying what is most important to you and your organization. Make sure everyone understands what these values and principles are, and how they guide your behavior and decision-making.

2   Model integrity: Model integrity by demonstrating honest and ethical behavior in all your interactions. Make sure your team sees you as a role model for integrity, and that they understand the importance of doing the right thing, even when it's difficult.

3   Communicate effectively: Communicate the importance of integrity effectively to your team and stakeholders. Make sure everyone understands why integrity is important, and how it promotes a positive and productive work environment.

4   Hold yourself and others accountable: Hold yourself and others accountable for adhering to the values and principles of integrity. Make sure everyone understands the consequences of violating these values and principles, and that they take ownership of their actions and decisions.

5   Foster a culture of integrity: Foster a culture of integrity within your organization by promoting ethical behavior, providing training and support, and recognizing and rewarding employees who demonstrate integrity.

Examples of Leading with Integrity

Here are some examples of leading with integrity:

1   Warren Buffett: Warren Buffett is known for his commitment to integrity in business. He has built a reputation for ethical behavior and honesty, and has been recognized as one of the most respected business leaders in the world.

2   Indra Nooyi: Indra Nooyi, the former CEO of PepsiCo, is known for her commitment to integrity and ethical behavior. She has been recognized for promoting a culture of integrity within her organization, and for her leadership in promoting sustainability and diversity.

3   Howard Schultz: Howard Schultz, the former CEO of Starbucks, is known for his commitment to integrity and ethical behavior. He has been recognized for his leadership in promoting social responsibility and sustainability, and for his efforts to build a culture of integrity within his organization.

Conclusion

Leading with integrity is an essential component of effective leadership. By following the steps outlined in this chapter, you can lead with integrity and develop a culture of integrity within your organization. Remember to define your values and principles, model integrity, communicate effectively, hold yourself and others accountable, and foster a culture of integrity. With these principles in mind, you can lead your organization towards success and achieve your vision and mission. Leading with integrity takes time, effort, and patience, but the payoff in terms of team performance, stakeholder trust, and overall success is well worth it.

CHAPTER 11:
EMPOWERING OTHERS

Empowering others is an essential component of effective leadership. It involves providing individuals and teams with the tools, resources, and support they need to take ownership of their work, make decisions, and contribute to the success of the organization. In this chapter, we'll explore the key principles of empowering others, and how to create a culture of empowerment within your organization.

What is Empowerment?

Empowerment is the process of providing individuals and teams with the tools, resources, and support they need to take ownership of their work, make decisions, and contribute to the success of the organization. It involves giving people the freedom to act and make decisions, and trusting them to do so.

Why is Empowerment Important?

Empowerment is important for several reasons. First, it can increase job satisfaction and motivation by giving individuals and teams a sense of ownership and autonomy over their work. Second, it can promote innovation and creativity by encouraging individuals and teams to share ideas and take risks. Finally, empowerment can help organizations achieve their goals by enabling them to tap into the full potential of their employees.

How to Empower Others?

Empowering others requires a thoughtful and intentional approach. Here are some steps to follow:

1   Define clear goals and expectations: Define clear goals and expectations for individuals and teams, and make sure they understand what they are working towards.

2   Provide tools and resources: Provide individuals and teams with the tools and resources they need to be successful. This can include training, technology, and access to information.

3   Encourage decision-making: Encourage individuals and teams to make decisions and take ownership of their work. Make sure they understand the consequences of their decisions, and provide support and guidance as needed.

4   Provide feedback and recognition: Provide individuals and teams with feedback and recognition for their work. Make sure they understand how their work contributes to the success of the organization, and recognize and reward their achievements.

5   Foster collaboration: Foster collaboration within and between teams by providing opportunities for individuals and teams to work together on projects and initiatives.

Examples of Empowering Others

Here are some examples of empowering others:

1   Google: Google is known for its culture of empowerment, where employees are encouraged to take risks, make decisions, and innovate. The company provides employees with the tools and resources they need to be successful, and fosters a culture of collaboration and innovation.

2   Zappos: Zappos is known for its culture of empowerment, where employees are given the freedom to make decisions and take ownership of their work. The company provides employees with the tools and resources they need to be successful, and fosters a culture of trust and transparency.

3   Southwest Airlines: Southwest Airlines is known for its culture of empowerment, where employees are encouraged to make decisions and take ownership of their work. The company provides employees with the training and support they need to be successful, and fosters a culture of collaboration and innovation.

Conclusion

Empowering others is an essential component of effective leadership. By following the steps outlined in this chapter, you can create a culture of empowerment within your organization and tap into the full potential of your employees. Remember to define clear goals and expectations, provide tools and resources, encourage decision-making, provide feedback and recognition, and foster collaboration. With these principles in mind, you can lead your organization towards success and achieve your vision and mission. Empowering others takes time, effort, and patience, but the payoff in terms of employee motivation, innovation, and overall success is well worth it.

CHAPTER 12: DEVELOPING
LEADERSHIP SKILLS

Developing leadership skills is an ongoing process that requires dedication, self-reflection, and a willingness to learn and grow. Effective leaders are continually seeking opportunities to develop and refine their skills, and to become better equipped to lead their teams towards success. In this chapter, we'll explore the key principles of developing leadership skills, and how to cultivate a growth mindset that will enable you to become a more effective leader.

What are Leadership Skills?

Leadership skills are the qualities and abilities that enable individuals to lead and manage others effectively. These skills include communication, problem-solving, decision-making, time management, and teamwork, among others. Effective leaders are able to leverage these skills to motivate and inspire their teams, and to achieve their organization's goals.

Why is Developing Leadership Skills Important?

Developing leadership skills is important for several reasons. First, it can increase your effectiveness as a leader by enabling you to make better decisions, communicate more effectively, and manage your time more efficiently. Second, it can promote a culture of growth and learning within your organization, by encouraging others to develop their own leadership skills. Finally, developing leadership skills can help you achieve your personal and professional goals, and enable you to become a more effective and successful leader.

How to Develop Leadership Skills?

Developing leadership skills requires a thoughtful and intentional approach. Here are some steps to follow:

1   Identify your strengths and weaknesses: Identify your strengths and weaknesses as a leader by reflecting on your past experiences and seeking feedback from others. Make sure you understand what you do well and what you need to work on.

2   Set goals for development: Set goals for your leadership development by identifying areas you want to improve and specific actions you can take to achieve your goals. Make sure your goals are measurable and achievable.

3   Seek out learning opportunities: Seek out learning opportunities that can help you develop your leadership skills. This can include reading books and articles, attending conferences and workshops, and seeking out mentorship and coaching.

4   Practice, practice, practice: Practice your leadership skills in a variety of settings, including at work, in volunteer or community organizations, and in your personal life. Make sure you are constantly seeking opportunities to apply and refine your skills.

5   Reflect on your experiences: Reflect on your experiences as a leader, and learn from your successes and failures. Make sure you are regularly seeking feedback from others, and using this feedback to inform your development.

Examples of Developing Leadership Skills

Here are some examples of developing leadership skills:

1   Barack Obama: Barack Obama, the former president of the United States, is known for his commitment to leadership

development. He regularly sought out feedback from his team and other leaders, and was known for his ability to learn and adapt in response to changing circumstances.

2   Elon Musk: Elon Musk, the CEO of SpaceX and Tesla, is known for his commitment to learning and growth. He regularly reads books and articles on leadership and innovation, and is constantly seeking out new learning opportunities to develop his skills.

3   Sheryl Sandberg: Sheryl Sandberg, the COO of Facebook, is known for her commitment to leadership development, and has written extensively on the subject in her book, "Lean In." She regularly seeks out mentorship and coaching, and is constantly seeking out opportunities to develop her skills as a leader.

Conclusion

Developing leadership skills is an essential component of effective leadership. By following the steps outlined in this chapter, you can cultivate a growth mindset that will enable you to become a more effective and successful leader. Remember to identify your strengths and weaknesses, set goals for development, seek out learning opportunities, practice your skills, and reflect on your experiences. With these principles in mind, you can lead your organization towards success and achieve your vision and mission. Developing leadership skills takes time, effort, and patience, but the payoff in terms of personal and professional growth, and the ability to lead others towards success, is well worth it. By continually seeking out new opportunities for growth and development, you can become the best leader possible, and inspire your team to achieve great things.

CHAPTER 13:
MANAGING CHANGE

Managing change is a critical component of effective leadership. Change is inevitable in any organization, and it is the leader's responsibility to manage this change in a way that promotes positive outcomes and minimizes negative impacts. In this chapter, we'll explore the key principles of managing change, and how to develop a change management plan that will enable you to lead your team through any organizational change.

What is Change Management?

Change management is the process of planning, implementing, and managing changes within an organization. It involves identifying the need for change, communicating the change to stakeholders, and developing a plan to ensure a smooth transition to the new state.

Why is Change Management Important?

Change management is important for several reasons. First, it can minimize resistance to change by engaging stakeholders and communicating the reasons for the change. Second, it can ensure that the change is implemented smoothly and effectively, minimizing the impact on the organization's operations. Finally, change management can promote a culture of adaptability and flexibility within the organization, enabling it to respond to changing market conditions and other external factors.

How to Manage Change?

Managing change requires a thoughtful and intentional approach. Here are some steps to follow:

1   Identify the need for change: Identify the need for change by assessing the organization's performance and identifying areas where improvements can be made. Make sure you understand the reasons for the change and the potential impacts on the organization.

2   Develop a change management plan: Develop a change management plan that outlines the goals, objectives, and timeline for the change. Make sure you identify the stakeholders who will be affected by the change, and develop a communication plan to ensure that they are informed and engaged throughout the process.

3   Communicate the change: Communicate the change to stakeholders, including employees, customers, and other key stakeholders. Make sure you explain the reasons for the change, the goals and objectives, and the potential impacts on the organization.

4   Implement the change: Implement the change according to the plan, making sure to monitor progress and adjust the plan as needed. Make sure you provide support and resources to stakeholders throughout the process, and address any concerns or issues that arise.

5   Evaluate the change: Evaluate the change to determine its effectiveness, and identify areas where improvements can be made. Make sure you collect feedback from stakeholders and use this feedback to inform future change management initiatives.

Examples of Managing Change

Here are some examples of managing change:

1   Apple: Apple is known for its ability to manage change effectively, including its transition from a computer company to a mobile device company. The company has a strong culture of innovation and flexibility, which enables it to respond to changing market conditions and evolving customer needs.

2   IBM: IBM is known for its ability to manage change, including its transformation from a hardware company to a software and services company. The company has a strong focus on innovation and collaboration, which enables it to adapt to changing market conditions and emerging technologies.

3   Microsoft: Microsoft is known for its ability to manage change, including its shift from a desktop software company to a cloud-based services company. The company has a strong culture of innovation and customer focus, which enables it to respond to changing customer needs and emerging technologies.

Conclusion

Managing change is an essential component of effective leadership. By following the steps outlined in this chapter, you can develop a change management plan that will enable you to lead your team through any organizational change. Remember to identify the need for change, develop a change management plan, communicate the change, implement the change, and evaluate the change. With these principles in mind, you can lead your organization towards success and achieve your vision and mission. Managing change takes time, effort, and patience, but the payoff in terms of a more adaptable and flexible organization is well worth it. By embracing change management, you can ensure that your organization is able to respond to changing market conditions and emerging technologies, and that you are able to lead your team towards success in any situation. With the right approach, change can be a positive force for growth and improvement, and can help your organization achieve its goals and thrive in an ever-changing business environment.

CHAPTER 14: BUILDING
A POSITIVE CULTURE

Building a positive culture is an essential component of effective leadership. A positive culture can promote employee satisfaction, productivity, and engagement, and can help your organization achieve its goals. In this chapter, we'll explore the key principles of building a positive culture, and how to create a culture that supports and inspires your team.

What is Culture?

Culture refers to the shared values, beliefs, and behaviors that define an organization. It includes the way people interact with each other, the way decisions are made, and the way work is accomplished. Culture can have a significant impact on the success of an organization, and can influence employee satisfaction, productivity, and engagement.

Why is Building a Positive Culture Important?

Building a positive culture is important for several reasons. First, it can promote employee satisfaction and engagement, which can lead to higher levels of productivity and performance. Second, it can promote a sense of belonging and community within the organization, which can help retain employees and reduce turnover. Finally, a positive culture can help promote ethical behavior, and can help the organization achieve its goals in a responsible and sustainable way.

How to Build a Positive Culture?

Building a positive culture requires a thoughtful and intentional approach. Here are some steps to follow:

1   Define the culture: Define the culture you want to create, and make sure everyone in the organization understands and embraces it. This can include identifying the values and behaviors you want to promote, and developing a set of guiding principles that will inform decision-making and behavior.

2   Lead by example: Leaders must set an example for the rest of the organization by modeling the values and behaviors they want to promote. Make sure you are living up to the values and behaviors you want to see in others, and hold yourself and others accountable for maintaining the culture.

3   Communicate the culture: Communicate the culture to employees and stakeholders, and make sure they understand the values and behaviors that are expected of them. This can include regular communication, training, and reinforcement.

4   Hire for cultural fit: When hiring new employees, make sure they are a good fit for the culture you are trying to create. This can involve assessing their values and behaviors during the hiring process, and making sure they understand and embrace the culture.

5   Celebrate successes: Celebrate successes that are aligned with the culture, and recognize individuals and teams who are exemplifying the values and behaviors you want to promote. Make sure you are regularly recognizing and rewarding positive contributions.

Examples of Building a Positive Culture

Here are some examples of building a positive culture:

1   Zappos: Zappos is known for its positive culture, which is focused on customer service, employee empowerment, and a fun and engaging workplace. The company promotes a strong sense of community and belonging, and regularly celebrates successes that are aligned with its culture.

2   Patagonia: Patagonia is known for its positive culture, which is focused on environmental sustainability, social responsibility, and employee well-being. The company promotes a strong sense of purpose and responsibility, and regularly celebrates successes that are aligned with its values.

3   Southwest Airlines: Southwest Airlines is known for its positive culture, which is focused on employee empowerment, customer service, and a fun and engaging workplace. The company promotes a strong sense of community and belonging, and regularly celebrates successes that are aligned with its culture.

Conclusion

Building a positive culture is an essential component of effective leadership. By following the steps outlined in this chapter, you can create a culture that supports and inspires your team, and helps your organization achieve its goals. Remember to define the culture, lead by example, communicate the culture, hire for cultural fit, and celebrate successes. With these principles in mind, you can create a positive and engaging workplace that promotes employee satisfaction, productivity, and engagement, and that helps your organization thrive. Building a positive culture takes time, effort, and patience, but the payoff in terms of a more engaged and productive workforce is well worth it. By prioritizing culture as a key component of your leadership strategy, you can build a strong and sustainable organization that can weather any challenge and achieve great things.

CHAPTER 15:
BEING ADAPTABLE

Being adaptable is a critical component of effective leadership. The ability to adapt to changing circumstances and environments is essential for success in today's fast-paced business world. In this chapter, we'll explore the key principles of being adaptable, and how to develop a mindset that enables you to respond to change and uncertainty.

What is Adaptability?

Adaptability is the ability to adjust and thrive in changing circumstances and environments. It involves being flexible, open-minded, and willing to learn and grow. Adaptable leaders are able to respond to changing market conditions, emerging technologies, and evolving customer needs, and are able to lead their teams towards success in any situation.

Why is Adaptability Important?

Adaptability is important for several reasons. First, it can enable you to respond to changing market conditions and emerging technologies, and to stay ahead of the competition. Second, it can promote a culture of innovation and creativity within your organization, by encouraging others to be open-minded and flexible. Finally, being adaptable can help you achieve your personal and professional goals, and enable you to become a more effective and successful leader.

How to Be Adaptable?

Being adaptable requires a thoughtful and intentional approach. Here are some steps to follow:

1   Embrace change: Embrace change as an opportunity for growth and development. Make sure you are open-minded and willing to learn, and that you are constantly seeking out new opportunities for growth and development.
2   Be flexible: Be flexible in your approach to work, and be willing to adjust your plans and strategies as needed. Make sure you are able to pivot quickly in response to changing circumstances, and that you are able to lead your team towards success in any situation.
3   Stay informed: Stay informed about emerging trends, technologies, and market conditions, and make sure you are constantly seeking out new information and insights. Make sure you are able to adapt to changing circumstances, and that you are able to lead your team towards success in any situation.
4   Be resilient: Be resilient in the face of challenges and setbacks, and make sure you are able to bounce back quickly from adversity. Make sure you are able to persevere in the face of uncertainty, and that you are able to inspire and motivate your team towards success.
5   Develop a growth mindset: Develop a growth mindset that enables you to view challenges and setbacks as opportunities for growth and development. Make sure you are able to learn from your experiences, and that you are able to apply these lessons to future situations.

Examples of Being Adaptable

Here are some examples of being adaptable:

1   Jeff Bezos: Jeff Bezos, the founder of Amazon, is known for

his ability to be adaptable in response to changing market conditions and emerging technologies. He has continually pivoted Amazon's business model in response to changing market conditions, and has created a culture of innovation and flexibility within the organization.

2   Satya Nadella: Satya Nadella, the CEO of Microsoft, is known for his ability to be adaptable in response to changing market conditions and emerging technologies. He has led Microsoft's transformation from a desktop software company to a cloud-based services company, and has created a culture of innovation and customer focus within the organization.

3   Elon Musk: Elon Musk, the CEO of SpaceX and Tesla, is known for his ability to be adaptable in response to changing market conditions and emerging technologies. He has continually pivoted his business models in response to changing market conditions, and has created a culture of innovation and flexibility within his organizations.

Conclusion

Being adaptable is an essential component of effective leadership. By following the steps outlined in this chapter, you can develop a mindset that enables you to respond to change and uncertainty, and to lead your team towards success in any situation. Remember to embrace change, be flexible, stay informed, be resilient, and develop a growth mindset. With these principles in mind, you can become a more adaptable and effective leader, and inspire your team to achieve great things. Being adaptable takes time, effort, and patience, but the payoff in terms of personal and professional growth, and the ability to lead others towards success, is well worth it. By continually seeking out new opportunities for growth and development, you can become the best leader possible, and inspire your team to achieve great things.

CHAPTER 16: BALANCING
WORK AND LIFE

Balancing work and life is an important component of effective leadership. The ability to manage your time and priorities effectively is essential for maintaining a healthy and fulfilling life outside of work, and for avoiding burnout and exhaustion. In this chapter, we'll explore the key principles of balancing work and life, and how to create a life that is both productive and fulfilling.

Why is Balancing Work and Life Important?

Balancing work and life is important for several reasons. First, it can help you avoid burnout and exhaustion, and can promote a healthier and more sustainable lifestyle. Second, it can promote personal and professional growth, by allowing you to pursue interests and activities outside of work that can enrich your life and help you achieve your goals. Finally, it can help you become a more effective and successful leader, by promoting a healthy work-life balance that enables you to be productive and focused both at work and at home.

How to Balance Work and Life?

Balancing work and life requires a thoughtful and intentional approach. Here are some steps to follow:

1   Set priorities: Set priorities for your work and your life, and make sure you are clear about what is most important to you. This can involve creating a list of goals and priorities

for both your personal and professional life, and regularly reviewing and updating this list to ensure that you are staying focused and aligned with your values.

2   Manage your time effectively: Manage your time effectively, and make sure you are setting aside time for both work and non-work activities. This can involve creating a schedule or calendar that includes time for work, family, friends, and personal interests, and regularly reviewing and updating this schedule to ensure that you are using your time effectively.

3   Set boundaries: Set boundaries between your work and personal life, and make sure you are able to disconnect from work and recharge outside of working hours. This can involve setting limits on when you will respond to emails or phone calls, and setting aside time for relaxation, hobbies, and other non-work activities.

4   Practice self-care: Practice self-care, and make sure you are taking care of your physical, emotional, and mental health. This can involve exercise, healthy eating, mindfulness practices, and other activities that promote relaxation and well-being.

5   Delegate: Delegate tasks and responsibilities to others, and make sure you are able to rely on your team to help you manage your workload. This can involve identifying areas where you can delegate tasks, and regularly communicating with your team to ensure that everyone is on the same page.

Examples of Balancing Work and Life

Here are some examples of balancing work and life:

1   Oprah Winfrey: Oprah Winfrey is known for her ability to balance her work and personal life, and for her commitment to self-care and personal growth. She regularly takes time off to relax and recharge, and is

committed to maintaining a healthy work-life balance.

2   Sheryl Sandberg: Sheryl Sandberg, the COO of Facebook, is known for her ability to balance her work and personal life, and for her commitment to mentoring and supporting other women in the workplace. She regularly takes time off to spend with her family, and is committed to promoting a healthy work-life balance for all employees.

3   Bill Gates: Bill Gates, the co-founder of Microsoft, is known for his ability to balance his work and personal life, and for his commitment to philanthropy and social responsibility. He regularly takes time off to focus on his charitable activities, and is committed to using his wealth and influence to make a positive impact on the world.

Conclusion

Balancing work and life is an essential component of effective leadership. By following the steps outlined in this chapter, you can create a life that is both productive and fulfilling, and that enables you to achieve your personal and professional goals. Remember to set priorities, manage your time effectively, set boundaries, practice self-care, and delegate. With these principles in mind, you can become a more effective and successful leader, and create a life that is both rewarding and fulfilling. Balancing work and life takes time, effort, and patience, but the payoff in terms of personal and professional growth, and the ability to live a more satisfying and fulfilling life, is well worth it. By prioritizing work-life balance as a key component of your leadership strategy, you can become the best leader possible, and inspire your team to achieve great things.

CHAPTER 17:
BUILDING RESILIENCE

Building resilience is an important component of effective leadership. The ability to bounce back from challenges and setbacks, and to persevere in the face of adversity, is essential for achieving personal and professional success. In this chapter, we'll explore the key principles of building resilience, and how to develop a mindset that enables you to overcome obstacles and achieve your goals.

What is Resilience?

Resilience is the ability to bounce back from challenges and setbacks, and to persevere in the face of adversity. It involves being able to adapt to changing circumstances, and to maintain a positive and focused mindset even in difficult situations. Resilient leaders are able to overcome obstacles and achieve their goals, and are able to inspire and motivate their team towards success.

Why is Resilience Important?

Resilience is important for several reasons. First, it can enable you to overcome challenges and setbacks, and to persevere in the face of adversity. This can help you achieve your personal and professional goals, and can promote personal and professional growth. Second, it can promote a culture of resilience and perseverance within your organization, by encouraging others to adopt a similar mindset. Finally, being resilient can help you become a more effective and successful leader, by enabling you to inspire and motivate your team towards success, even in difficult situations.

How to Build Resilience?

Building resilience requires a thoughtful and intentional approach. Here are some steps to follow:

1   Develop a growth mindset: Develop a growth mindset that enables you to view challenges and setbacks as opportunities for growth and development. Make sure you are able to learn from your experiences, and that you are able to apply these lessons to future situations.
2   Practice mindfulness: Practice mindfulness, and make sure you are able to maintain a positive and focused mindset even in difficult situations. This can involve meditation, deep breathing, and other techniques that promote relaxation and focus.
3   Seek support: Seek support from others, and make sure you are able to rely on your team and your network for help and guidance. This can involve seeking out mentors, coaches, or peers who can offer advice and support when you need it.
4   Take care of your physical and emotional health: Take care of your physical and emotional health, and make sure you are able to manage stress effectively. This can involve exercise, healthy eating, sleep, and other activities that promote relaxation and well-being.
5   Celebrate successes: Celebrate your successes, and make sure you are able to acknowledge and appreciate your accomplishments. This can help you maintain a positive and optimistic mindset, even in the face of challenges and setbacks.

Examples of Building Resilience

Here are some examples of building resilience:

1   Nelson Mandela: Nelson Mandela, the former president of South Africa, is known for his resilience and perseverance in the face of adversity. He spent 27 years in prison, but was able to maintain a positive and focused mindset, and to emerge from prison as a leader and inspiration to others.

2   Serena Williams: Serena Williams, the professional tennis player, is known for her resilience and perseverance in the face of injury and setbacks. She has overcome numerous injuries and setbacks throughout her career, and has maintained a positive and focused mindset, enabling her to achieve great success.

3   Steve Jobs: Steve Jobs, the co-founder of Apple, is known for his resilience and perseverance in the face of challenges and setbacks. He was fired from Apple in 1985, but was able to bounce back and eventually return to lead the company to great success.

Conclusion

Building resilience is an essential component of effective leadership. By following the steps outlined in this chapter, you can develop a mindset that enables you to overcome obstacles and achieve your goals, and to inspire and motivate your team towards success. Remember to develop a growth mindset, practice mindfulness, seek support, take care of your physical and emotional health, and celebrate successes. With these principles in mind, you can become a more effective and successful leader, and inspire your team to achieve great things. Building resilience takes time, effort, and patience, but the payoff in terms of personal and professional growth, and the ability to lead others towards success, is well worth it. By continually seeking out new opportunities for growth and development, you can become the best leader possible, and inspire your team to achieve great things.

CHAPTER 18: ENCOURAGING LEARNING AND DEVELOPMENT

Encouraging learning and development is an important component of effective leadership. The ability to inspire and motivate your team towards growth and development, and to create a culture of continuous learning and improvement, is essential for achieving personal and professional success. In this chapter, we'll explore the key principles of encouraging learning and development, and how to create a culture of growth and development within your organization.

Why is Encouraging Learning and Development Important?

Encouraging learning and development is important for several reasons. First, it can help you and your team achieve personal and professional growth, by enabling you to acquire new skills, knowledge, and perspectives. Second, it can promote innovation and creativity within your organization, by encouraging employees to think outside of the box and to pursue new ideas and approaches. Finally, it can help you become a more effective and successful leader, by creating a culture of continuous learning and improvement that enables you and your team to stay ahead of the curve.

How to Encourage Learning and Development?

Encouraging learning and development requires a thoughtful and intentional approach. Here are some steps to follow:

1   Set the example: Set the example by demonstrating a commitment to learning and development yourself. This can involve pursuing new skills, knowledge, and perspectives, and regularly sharing what you've learned with your team.

2   Create a culture of learning: Create a culture of learning within your organization, by encouraging your team to pursue new ideas and approaches, and by celebrating successes and achievements. This can involve setting goals and targets for growth and development, and providing opportunities for learning and development, such as workshops, conferences, and training programs.

3   Provide feedback: Provide feedback to your team, and make sure you are able to help them identify areas for growth and development. This can involve regular check-ins and performance reviews, and providing guidance and support as needed.

4   Foster collaboration: Foster collaboration within your organization, and make sure your team is able to work together effectively towards common goals. This can involve creating opportunities for brainstorming, problem-solving, and idea-sharing, and regularly checking in with your team to ensure that everyone is on the same page.

5   Encourage experimentation: Encourage experimentation and risk-taking within your organization, and make sure your team is able to pursue new ideas and approaches without fear of failure. This can involve creating a culture that celebrates experimentation and innovation, and providing resources and support for employees who want to pursue new ideas.

Examples of Encouraging Learning and Development

Here are some examples of encouraging learning and development:

1 Google: Google is known for its commitment to learning and development, and for its innovative approach to employee training and development. The company provides opportunities for employees to pursue new skills and knowledge, and regularly celebrates successes and achievements.

2 Amazon: Amazon is known for its culture of innovation and experimentation, and for its commitment to helping employees grow and develop. The company provides training and development opportunities, and encourages employees to pursue new ideas and approaches.

3 Microsoft: Microsoft is known for its collaborative and supportive culture, and for its commitment to creating opportunities for growth and development. The company provides resources and support for employees who want to pursue new skills and knowledge, and encourages experimentation and risk-taking.

Conclusion

Encouraging learning and development is an essential component of effective leadership. By following the steps outlined in this chapter, you can create a culture of growth and development within your organization, and inspire and motivate your team towards success. Remember to set the example, create a culture of learning, provide feedback, foster collaboration, and encourage experimentation. With these principles in mind, you can become a more effective and successful leader, and create an organization that is capable of achieving great things. Encouraging learning and development takes time, effort, and patience, but the payoff in terms of personal and professional growth, and the ability to lead others towards success, is well worth it. By continually seeking out new opportunities for growth and development, you can become the best leader possible, and inspire your team to achieve great things. Encouraging learning and development is a journey, and one that requires ongoing commitment and dedication. But by embracing this approach to leadership, you can create a culture of growth and development that will enable you and your team to achieve great things, and to continue growing and improving over time.

CHAPTER 19: LEADING
WITH EMOTIONAL INTELLIGENCE

Leading with emotional intelligence is an important component of effective leadership. The ability to understand and manage your own emotions, and to empathize with and respond to the emotions of others, is essential for building strong relationships and inspiring and motivating your team towards success. In this chapter, we'll explore the key principles of leading with emotional intelligence, and how to develop a mindset that enables you to connect with and inspire your team.

What is Emotional Intelligence?

Emotional intelligence is the ability to understand and manage your own emotions, and to empathize with and respond to the emotions of others. It involves being able to read and interpret the emotions of others, and to respond to them in a way that is thoughtful and appropriate. Emotional intelligence is an essential component of effective leadership, and can help you build strong relationships with your team, and inspire and motivate them towards success.

Why is Emotional Intelligence Important?

Emotional intelligence is important for several reasons. First, it can help you build strong relationships with your team, by enabling you to connect with them on an emotional level, and to understand and respond to their needs and concerns. Second, it can promote a positive and supportive culture within your organization, by encouraging empathy and compassion towards others. Finally, it can help you become a more effective and successful leader, by enabling you to inspire and motivate your team towards success.

How to Lead with Emotional Intelligence?

Leading with emotional intelligence requires a thoughtful and intentional approach. Here are some steps to follow:

1   Develop self-awareness: Develop self-awareness, and make sure you are able to understand and manage your own emotions. This can involve reflecting on your own emotions, and practicing techniques that promote self-awareness, such as meditation, deep breathing, or journaling.

2   Practice empathy: Practice empathy, and make sure you are able to understand and respond to the emotions of others. This can involve actively listening to your team, and taking the time to understand their needs and concerns.

3   Foster a positive culture: Foster a positive and supportive culture within your organization, and make sure your team feels valued and supported. This can involve providing resources and support for employees, and creating a culture that celebrates empathy and compassion towards others.

4   Communicate effectively: Communicate effectively with your team, and make sure you are able to convey your ideas and goals in a way that is clear and understandable. This can involve practicing active listening, and making sure you are able to respond to the needs and concerns of your team.

5   Manage conflicts: Manage conflicts effectively, and make sure you are able to resolve disagreements in a way that is thoughtful and constructive. This can involve practicing techniques that promote conflict resolution, such as active listening, empathy, and compromise.

Examples of Leading with Emotional Intelligence

Here are some examples of leading with emotional intelligence:

1   Oprah Winfrey: Oprah Winfrey is known for her ability to connect with others on an emotional level, and for her commitment to empathy and compassion towards others. She has created a positive and supportive culture within her organization, and has inspired and motivated millions of people through her work.

2   Satya Nadella: Satya Nadella, the CEO of Microsoft, is known for his commitment to empathy and emotional intelligence. He has created a culture of collaboration and innovation within the organization, and has inspired and motivated his team towards success.

3   Melinda Gates: Melinda Gates, the philanthropist and businesswoman, is known for her ability to connect with others and to empathize with their needs and concerns. She has inspired and motivated her team towards achieving great things, and has created a culture of empathy and compassion within her organization.

Conclusion

Leading with emotional intelligence is an essential component of effective leadership. By following the steps outlined in this chapter, you can develop the mindset and skills needed to connect with and inspire your team towards success. Remember to develop self-awareness, practice empathy, foster a positive culture, communicate effectively, and manage conflicts thoughtfully. With these principles in mind, you can become a more effective and successful leader, and create an organization that is capable of achieving great things. Leading with emotional intelligence takes time, effort, and patience, but the payoff in terms of personal and professional growth, and the ability to lead others towards success, is well worth it. By continually seeking out new opportunities for growth and development, you can become the best leader possible, and inspire your team to achieve great things.

CHAPTER 20: MANAGING
TIME AND PRIORITIES

Managing time and priorities is an essential component of effective leadership. The ability to prioritize tasks and manage your time effectively is essential for achieving personal and professional success, and for leading your team towards success. In this chapter, we'll explore the key principles of managing time and priorities, and how to develop a mindset that enables you to be productive and focused.

Why is Managing Time and Priorities Important?

Managing time and priorities is important for several reasons. First, it can help you achieve personal and professional growth, by enabling you to focus on the most important tasks and achieve your goals. Second, it can promote a positive and productive culture within your organization, by encouraging employees to manage their time effectively and to prioritize their work. Finally, it can help you become a more effective and successful leader, by enabling you to inspire and motivate your team towards success.

How to Manage Time and Priorities?

Managing time and priorities requires a thoughtful and intentional approach. Here are some steps to follow:

1   Prioritize your tasks: Prioritize your tasks, and make sure you are able to focus on the most important ones. This can involve creating a to-do list, and ranking your tasks in order

of importance.

2   Set goals: Set goals for yourself and your team, and make sure you are able to achieve them in a timely and effective manner. This can involve creating SMART goals that are specific, measurable, achievable, relevant, and time-bound.

3   Use a schedule: Use a schedule to manage your time effectively, and make sure you are able to allocate your time to the most important tasks. This can involve using a planner, calendar, or time management app to keep track of your schedule.

4   Minimize distractions: Minimize distractions, and make sure you are able to focus on your work. This can involve turning off notifications, working in a quiet space, or using techniques such as the Pomodoro Technique to help you stay focused.

5   Delegate tasks: Delegate tasks to your team, and make sure you are able to focus on the most important tasks. This can involve identifying tasks that can be delegated, and providing clear instructions and guidance to your team.

Examples of Managing Time and Priorities

Here are some examples of managing time and priorities:

1   Warren Buffet: Warren Buffet, the billionaire investor and businessman, is known for his ability to manage his time effectively and to prioritize his work. He has a clear schedule and a disciplined approach to managing his time, and is able to achieve his goals in a timely and effective manner.

2   Tim Cook: Tim Cook, the CEO of Apple, is known for his ability to delegate tasks effectively and to prioritize his work. He is able to focus on the most important tasks, and has created a culture of productivity and focus within the organization.

3   Indra Nooyi: Indra Nooyi, the former CEO of PepsiCo, is

known for her ability to set goals and to manage her time effectively. She has a disciplined approach to managing her time, and is able to achieve her goals in a timely and effective manner.

Conclusion

Managing time and priorities is an essential component of effective leadership. By following the steps outlined in this chapter, you can develop the mindset and skills needed to manage your time effectively, prioritize your work, and achieve your goals. Remember to prioritize your tasks, set goals, use a schedule, minimize distractions, and delegate tasks. With these principles in mind, you can become a more effective and successful leader, and create an organization that is capable of achieving great things. Managing time and priorities takes time, effort, and patience, but the payoff in terms of personal and professional growth, and the ability to lead others towards success, is well worth it.

CHAPTER 21: BEING
ACCOUNTABLE

Being accountable is an essential component of effective leadership. The ability to take responsibility for your actions, to hold yourself and your team accountable for their performance, and to learn from your mistakes, is essential for building trust and credibility with your team, and for inspiring and motivating them towards success. In this chapter, we'll explore the key principles of being accountable, and how to develop a mindset that enables you to take responsibility for your actions and hold yourself and your team accountable.

Why is Being Accountable Important?

Being accountable is important for several reasons. First, it can help you build trust and credibility with your team, by demonstrating your commitment to taking responsibility for your actions. Second, it can promote a culture of responsibility and accountability within your organization, by encouraging employees to take ownership of their work and to learn from their mistakes. Finally, it can help you become a more effective and successful leader, by enabling you to inspire and motivate your team towards success.

How to Be Accountable?

Being accountable requires a thoughtful and intentional approach. Here are some steps to follow:

1   Take responsibility: Take responsibility for your actions, and make sure you are able to admit when you make a mistake. This can involve acknowledging your mistakes, and taking the time to reflect on what went wrong.

2   Set clear expectations: Set clear expectations for yourself and your team, and make sure you are able to hold yourself and your team accountable for their performance. This can involve setting goals and objectives, and tracking progress towards those goals.

3   Communicate openly: Communicate openly with your team, and make sure you are able to discuss challenges and opportunities openly and honestly. This can involve soliciting feedback from your team, and using that feedback to improve your performance.

4   Learn from your mistakes: Learn from your mistakes, and make sure you are able to grow and develop as a leader. This can involve reflecting on your performance, and identifying areas for improvement.

5   Lead by example: Lead by example, and make sure you are able to demonstrate your commitment to being accountable. This can involve modeling responsible behavior for your team, and holding yourself to the same standards that you hold your team to.

Examples of Being Accountable

Here are some examples of being accountable:

1   Sheryl Sandberg: Sheryl Sandberg, the COO of Facebook, is known for her commitment to being accountable. She has taken responsibility for the company's missteps, and has worked to create a culture of accountability within the organization.

2   Elon Musk: Elon Musk, the CEO of Tesla and SpaceX, is known for his ability to take risks and to hold himself

and his team accountable for their performance. He has set ambitious goals for his companies, and has worked tirelessly to achieve those goals.

3   Ursula Burns: Ursula Burns, the former CEO of Xerox, is known for her ability to take responsibility for her actions and to hold herself and her team accountable. She has worked to create a culture of responsibility and accountability within the organization, and has inspired and motivated her team towards success.

Conclusion

Being accountable is an essential component of effective leadership. By following the steps outlined in this chapter, you can develop the mindset and skills needed to take responsibility for your actions, hold yourself and your team accountable, and learn from your mistakes. Remember to take responsibility, set clear expectations, communicate openly, learn from your mistakes, and lead by example. With these principles in mind, you can become a more effective and successful leader, and create an organization that is capable of achieving great things. Being accountable takes time, effort, and patience, but the payoff in terms of personal and professional growth, and the ability to lead others towards success, is well worth it.

CHAPTER 22: BUILDING A
DIVERSE AND INCLUSIVE TEAM

Building a diverse and inclusive team is an essential component of effective leadership. The ability to create a team that is representative of diverse backgrounds, experiences, and perspectives, and to foster an environment that is inclusive and welcoming to all, is essential for promoting innovation, creativity, and success. In this chapter, we'll explore the key principles of building a diverse and inclusive team, and how to develop a mindset that enables you to create a team that is capable of achieving great things.

Why is Building a Diverse and Inclusive Team Important?

Building a diverse and inclusive team is important for several reasons. First, it can promote innovation and creativity, by encouraging employees to bring their unique perspectives and experiences to the table. Second, it can create a culture of respect and inclusivity within your organization, by valuing and celebrating diversity. Finally, it can help you become a more effective and successful leader, by enabling you to inspire and motivate your team towards success.

How to Build a Diverse and Inclusive Team?

Building a diverse and inclusive team requires a thoughtful and intentional approach. Here are some steps to follow:

1   Be intentional: Be intentional about creating a diverse and

inclusive team, and make sure you are able to identify and address any barriers to diversity and inclusion. This can involve reviewing your hiring practices, and ensuring that they are inclusive and welcoming to all.

2   Value diversity: Value diversity and celebrate the unique perspectives and experiences that each employee brings to the team. This can involve creating opportunities for employees to share their experiences and perspectives, and to learn from one another.

3   Foster inclusivity: Foster an inclusive and welcoming environment within your organization, and make sure that every employee feels valued and supported. This can involve creating a culture of respect and inclusivity, and providing resources and support for employees who may be facing discrimination or bias.

4   Provide training: Provide training for your team on diversity and inclusion, and make sure that everyone understands the importance of creating a diverse and inclusive team. This can involve providing workshops or seminars on topics such as unconscious bias and cultural competence.

5   Lead by example: Lead by example, and make sure that you are able to model the behavior you expect from your team. This can involve demonstrating a commitment to diversity and inclusion, and holding yourself and your team accountable for creating a diverse and inclusive team.

Examples of Building a Diverse and Inclusive Team

Here are some examples of building a diverse and inclusive team:

1   Satya Nadella: Satya Nadella, the CEO of Microsoft, is known for his commitment to creating a diverse and inclusive team. He has worked to create a culture of inclusivity within the organization, and has set ambitious

goals for increasing the representation of women and people of color within the company.

2   Mellody Hobson: Mellody Hobson, the co-CEO of Ariel Investments, is known for her commitment to promoting diversity and inclusion within the financial industry. She has worked to create a culture of inclusivity within her organization, and has advocated for greater representation of women and people of color within the industry.

3   Sundar Pichai: Sundar Pichai, the CEO of Google, is known for his commitment to creating a diverse and inclusive team. He has worked to increase the representation of women and people of color within the company, and has created programs to support underrepresented communities.

Conclusion

Building a diverse and inclusive team is an essential component of effective leadership. By following the steps outlined in this chapter, you can develop the mindset and skills needed to create a team that is representative of diverse backgrounds, experiences, and perspectives, and to foster an environment that is inclusive and welcoming to all. Remember to be intentional, value diversity, foster inclusivity, provide training, and lead by example. By doing so, you can become a more effective and successful leader, and create an organization that is capable of achieving great things. Remember that building a diverse and inclusive team is an ongoing process that requires continuous effort and attention. But by making it a priority, you can create a team that is capable of achieving great things and making a positive impact in the world.

CHAPTER 23: LEADING
IN TIMES OF CRISIS

Leading in times of crisis is one of the most challenging aspects of leadership. Whether it's a global pandemic, an economic recession, a natural disaster, or a corporate scandal, crises can be overwhelming, stressful, and disruptive to your team and your organization. In this chapter, we'll explore the key principles of leading in times of crisis, and how to develop a mindset that enables you to navigate difficult times and emerge stronger and more resilient.

Why is Leading in Times of Crisis Important?

Leading in times of crisis is important for several reasons. First, it can help you build trust and credibility with your team, by demonstrating your commitment to leading through difficult times. Second, it can enable you to make tough decisions and take decisive action, even when the situation is uncertain or unpredictable. Finally, it can help you become a more effective and successful leader, by enabling you to inspire and motivate your team towards success, even in the face of adversity.

How to Lead in Times of Crisis?

Leading in times of crisis requires a thoughtful and intentional approach. Here are some steps to follow:

1   Communicate regularly: Communicate regularly with your team, and make sure you are able to provide them with

the information and support they need. This can involve providing regular updates on the situation, and being transparent and honest about the challenges you are facing.

2   Be decisive: Be decisive and take action, even when the situation is uncertain or unpredictable. This can involve making tough decisions, and taking responsibility for the consequences of those decisions.

3   Focus on priorities: Focus on the priorities that are most important to your team and your organization, and make sure you are able to allocate resources and energy towards those priorities. This can involve setting clear goals and objectives, and making sure that everyone is aligned around those goals.

4   Collaborate with others: Collaborate with others, both within and outside of your organization, and make sure you are able to draw on the expertise and resources of others. This can involve building partnerships, and working together to find solutions to the challenges you are facing.

5   Take care of yourself: Take care of yourself, and make sure you are able to manage your own stress and anxiety during times of crisis. This can involve taking breaks, practicing self-care, and seeking support when needed.

Examples of Leading in Times of Crisis

Here are some examples of leading in times of crisis:

1   Jacinda Ardern: Jacinda Ardern, the Prime Minister of New Zealand, is known for her leadership during the 2019 Christchurch mosque shootings. She demonstrated empathy and compassion for the victims and their families, and worked to unite the country in the wake of the tragedy.

2   Tim Cook: Tim Cook, the CEO of Apple, is known for his leadership during the COVID-19 pandemic. He made tough decisions to close Apple stores and offices, and shifted the

company's focus towards online sales and remote work.

3   Mary Barra: Mary Barra, the CEO of General Motors, is known for her leadership during the 2014 ignition switch recall crisis. She took decisive action to address the safety issues, and worked to rebuild trust with customers and investors.

Conclusion

Leading in times of crisis is one of the most challenging aspects of leadership, but it is also an opportunity to demonstrate your commitment to your team and your organization. By following the steps outlined in this chapter, you can develop the mindset and skills needed to navigate difficult times and emerge stronger and more resilient. Remember to communicate regularly, be decisive, focus on priorities, collaborate with others, and take care of yourself. By doing so, you can become a more effective and successful leader, and create an organization that is capable of achieving great things, even in the face of adversity. Remember that leading in times of crisis is an ongoing process that requires continuous effort and attention. But by making it a priority, you can create a team that is capable of achieving great things and making a positive impact in the world, even in the face of difficult circumstances. Leading in times of crisis can be a true test of your leadership skills, but it can also be an opportunity for growth, learning, and development. By embracing the challenges of crisis leadership, you can become a stronger, more effective, and more successful leader, and inspire your team to do the same.

CHAPTER 24:
CELEBRATING SUCCESS

As a leader, it's important to recognize and celebrate the successes of your team. Celebrating success not only provides a sense of accomplishment and satisfaction, but it also reinforces positive behavior, builds motivation, and enhances team cohesion. In this chapter, we'll explore the key principles of celebrating success, and how to develop a mindset that enables you to recognize and celebrate the successes of your team.

Why is Celebrating Success Important?

Celebrating success is important for several reasons. First, it provides a sense of accomplishment and satisfaction, and reinforces positive behavior. Second, it builds motivation and encourages team members to continue working towards their goals. Finally, it enhances team cohesion and strengthens relationships between team members.

How to Celebrate Success?

Celebrating success requires a thoughtful and intentional approach. Here are some steps to follow:

1   Set clear goals: Set clear and measurable goals for your team, and make sure everyone is aligned around those goals. This can involve creating a shared vision, and making sure that everyone understands how their work contributes to the success of the team.

2   Recognize individual contributions: Recognize the individual contributions of each team member, and make sure everyone feels valued and appreciated. This can involve providing regular feedback, and highlighting the strengths and accomplishments of each team member.

3   Create a culture of celebration: Create a culture of celebration within your organization, and make sure that success is celebrated and acknowledged. This can involve creating opportunities for team members to share their successes, and making sure that everyone is able to participate in the celebration.

4   Be authentic: Be authentic in your celebration, and make sure that you are able to genuinely appreciate the success of your team. This can involve expressing gratitude and excitement, and making sure that your celebration is consistent with your values and goals.

5   Learn from success: Learn from success, and use it as an opportunity to improve and grow. This can involve reflecting on the factors that contributed to success, and making sure that those factors are replicated in future projects.

Examples of Celebrating Success

Here are some examples of celebrating success:

1   Nike: Nike is known for its culture of celebration, and its commitment to recognizing and rewarding the successes of its employees. It provides regular recognition programs, and creates opportunities for employees to celebrate their successes together.

2   Google: Google is known for its emphasis on employee recognition, and its commitment to creating a culture of celebration. It provides regular recognition programs, and celebrates the successes of its employees in a variety

of ways, such as through company-wide meetings, social media, and internal communications.

3   Salesforce: Salesforce is known for its commitment to employee recognition, and its emphasis on celebrating success. It provides regular recognition programs, and encourages employees to celebrate their successes with their colleagues and managers.

Conclusion

Celebrating success is an essential component of effective leadership. By following the steps outlined in this chapter, you can develop the mindset and skills needed to recognize and celebrate the successes of your team. Remember to set clear goals, recognize individual contributions, create a culture of celebration, be authentic, and learn from success. By doing so, you can become a more effective and successful leader, and create a team that is capable of achieving great things and making a positive impact in the world. Remember that celebrating success is an ongoing process that requires continuous effort and attention. By making it a priority and consistently recognizing and celebrating the successes of your team, you can help foster a positive and productive work environment that encourages growth, development, and achievement. Celebrating success is not only important for building motivation and enhancing team cohesion, but it's also essential for creating a culture of positivity and appreciation. By embracing the principles of celebrating success, you can become a more effective and successful leader and inspire your team to reach new heights of achievement.

CHAPTER 25: CONTINUING
TO GROW AND LEARN

As a leader, it's important to recognize that growth and learning are ongoing processes. By continuing to learn and develop your skills, you can become a more effective and successful leader, and create a team that is capable of achieving great things. In this chapter, we'll explore the key principles of continuing to grow and learn, and how to develop a mindset that enables you to be a lifelong learner.

Why is Continuing to Grow and Learn Important?

Continuing to grow and learn is important for several reasons. First, it helps you stay relevant and up-to-date in a rapidly changing world. Second, it enables you to identify new opportunities for growth and development, and to capitalize on those opportunities. Finally, it helps you become a more effective and successful leader, by enhancing your skills, knowledge, and expertise.

How to Continue to Grow and Learn?

Continuing to grow and learn requires a thoughtful and intentional approach. Here are some steps to follow:

1   Identify your strengths and weaknesses: Identify your strengths and weaknesses, and make sure you are able to focus on areas of improvement. This can involve self-reflection, seeking feedback, and identifying areas where

you can improve.

2   Set clear goals: Set clear and measurable goals for your growth and development, and make sure you have a plan for achieving those goals. This can involve identifying specific skills or areas of knowledge you want to develop, and setting timelines and milestones for achieving those goals.

3   Seek out learning opportunities: Seek out learning opportunities, both within and outside of your organization, and make sure you are able to stay up-to-date on the latest trends and developments in your field. This can involve attending conferences, taking courses, reading books and articles, and seeking out mentorship and coaching.

4   Practice continuous improvement: Practice continuous improvement, and make sure you are always looking for ways to enhance your skills and knowledge. This can involve seeking out feedback, reflecting on your experiences, and making changes to your approach based on what you have learned.

5   Share your knowledge: Share your knowledge and expertise with others, and make sure you are able to contribute to the growth and development of your team. This can involve mentoring others, sharing your experiences and insights, and providing opportunities for others to learn and grow.

Examples of Continuing to Grow and Learn

Here are some examples of continuing to grow and learn:

1   Elon Musk: Elon Musk, the CEO of SpaceX and Tesla, is known for his commitment to lifelong learning. He reads extensively, attends conferences, and seeks out feedback and mentorship from others in his field.

2   Bill Gates: Bill Gates, the co-founder of Microsoft, is known

for his commitment to continuous improvement. He seeks out feedback, reflects on his experiences, and uses his knowledge and expertise to make a positive impact in the world.

3   Oprah Winfrey: Oprah Winfrey, the media mogul and philanthropist, is known for her commitment to personal growth and development. She seeks out mentorship and coaching, reads extensively, and practices continuous improvement in all aspects of her life.

Conclusion

Continuing to grow and learn is an essential component of effective leadership. By following the steps outlined in this chapter, you can develop the mindset and skills needed to be a lifelong learner. Remember to identify your strengths and weaknesses, set clear goals, seek out learning opportunities, practice continuous improvement, and share your knowledge with others. By doing so, you can become a more effective and successful leader, and create a team that is capable of achieving great things and making a positive impact in the world. Remember that continuing to grow and learn is a journey that requires continuous effort and attention. By making it a priority and consistently seeking out learning opportunities, you can become a more effective and successful leader, and create a team that is capable of achieving great things. As you continue to grow and learn, remember to stay open-minded, stay curious, and stay committed to the process of personal and professional development. By doing so, you can inspire your team to do the same, and create a positive and productive work environment that encourages growth, development, and achievement.

FINAL RECAP: BECOMING
A GREAT LEADER

Becoming a great leader is an ongoing process that requires continuous effort, dedication, and learning. In this book, we've explored the key principles of effective leadership, and how to develop the mindset and skills needed to be a successful and inspiring leader. We've discussed the importance of setting a vision, communicating effectively, building trust and collaboration, and leading with empathy and authenticity. We've also explored topics such as managing change, building a positive culture, and being adaptable in times of crisis.

Effective leadership is not something that can be learned overnight, and it's not a one-size-fits-all approach. Every leader is different, and every team is different. But by embracing the principles of effective leadership, and making a commitment to continuous growth and learning, you can become a more effective and successful leader, and create a team that is capable of achieving great things.

In conclusion, here are some key takeaways from this book:

1   Set a vision: Set a clear and inspiring vision for your team, and make sure everyone is aligned around that vision.
2   Communicate effectively: Communicate effectively with your team, and make sure everyone is able to share their ideas and perspectives.
3   Build trust and collaboration: Build trust and collaboration within your team, and make sure everyone feels valued and

appreciated.

4   Lead with empathy and authenticity: Lead with empathy and authenticity, and make sure you are able to connect with your team on a personal level.

5   Manage change: Manage change effectively, and make sure your team is able to adapt to new situations and challenges.

6   Build a positive culture: Build a positive culture within your organization, and make sure that everyone is able to thrive and grow.

7   Be adaptable: Be adaptable in times of crisis, and make sure you are able to lead your team through difficult situations.

8   Celebrate success: Celebrate the successes of your team, and make sure everyone feels valued and appreciated.

9   Continue to grow and learn: Continue to grow and learn, and make sure you are able to stay up-to-date on the latest trends and developments in your field.

Remember, becoming a great leader is a journey, not a destination. It requires continuous effort, dedication, and learning. By embracing the principles of effective leadership, and making a commitment to continuous growth and learning, you can become a more effective and successful leader, and inspire your team to reach new heights of achievement.

ACKNOWLEDGEMENT

I would like to express my heartfelt thanks to all the great leaders who have come before us, and who have inspired us with their wisdom, courage, and vision. Their legacies have paved the way for us to build upon their achievements, and to create a better world for future generations.

I would also like to thank the future leaders who are not yet born, but who will one day take up the mantle of leadership and carry the torch forward. Your dedication, passion, and commitment to making a positive impact in the world will be essential for creating a brighter future for all.

Finally, I would like to thank everyone who has supported me in the writing of this book, including my family, friends, and colleagues. Your encouragement, feedback, and insights have been invaluable, and I could not have done this without you.

To all the past, present, and future leaders of the world, I dedicate this book to you. May you be inspired to lead with courage, compassion, and vision, and may you leave a positive legacy that will endure for generations to come.